CAN GOD BE TRUSTED IN OUR TRIALS?

Tony Evans

MOODY PUBLISHERS
CHICAGO

All Scripture quotations, unless otherwise indicated, are taken from the
New American Standard Bible®, Copyright © The Lockman Foundation 1960,
1962, 1963, 1968, 1971, 1972, 1973, 1975, 1977, 1995. Used by permission.

Scripture quotations marked KJV are taken from the King James Version.

Library of Congress Cataloging-in-Publication Data

Evans, Anthony T.
    Can God be trusted in our trials? / Tony Evans.
        p. cm.
    ISBN 0-8024-4379-6
    1. Suffering—Religious aspects—Christianity. 2. Trust in God. I. Title.

BV4909.E83 2004
248.8'6—dc22

                                                                    2004001879

                        3 5 7 9 10 8 6 4 2

            Printed in the United States of America

CAN GOD BE TRUSTED IN OUR TRIALS?

CONTENTS

1

OUR
TRIALS
HAVE A
POSITIVE
PURPOSE

When I was growing up, I used to get irritated whenever my favorite television program was pre-empted by those tests of the Emergency Broadcast System, which would be used in case America was attacked or some other disaster occurred. When it was time for one of those tests, normal programming was interrupted, and a voice announced, "This is a test."

The nice thing about the television tests was that they only lasted about sixty seconds, and then normal programming resumed. Superman always caught the bad guys and rescued Lois Lane, and everything was cool.

But the Bible makes it inescapably clear that life's trials are not sixty-second interruptions, after which things return to normal and everything is cool again. That's why we need to learn the purpose God has in our trials, the spiritual resources He has given us to be victorious in any trial—and, maybe most important of all, His faithfulness to us throughout the process of enduring our trials.

Let me begin by offering a biblical definition of trials. Trials are adverse or negative circumstances that God either brings about directly or allows in order to develop us spiritually. Trials come in all sizes and colors: physical, financial, relational, emotional, and spiritual, just to name a few. The Bible's most comprehensive statement on life's trials teaches this foundational truth. The apostle James writes: "Consider it all joy, my brethren, when you encounter various trials, knowing that the testing of your faith produces endurance. And let endurance have its perfect result, so that you may be perfect and complete, lacking in nothing" (James 1:2–4).

There are several key concepts in these verses that we need to talk about, but the one that usually throws people is the Bible's command to count our trials as "all joy." That doesn't seem to make sense. How can we be joyful in the middle of a trial when everything is going wrong? Remember, trials by definition are negative circumstances. But God steps into the middle of our trials and tells us to be not just joyful but *overjoyed* that these things have come. How can we do this? We can do it because we know something important, which is explained in James 1:3–4.

As negative as our problems seem, they are always there for a positive reason, which is to develop us spiritually. God is not telling us to be joyful about the pain but about the purpose and the outcome of the pain, which is our spiritual completeness and maturity.

JOY VS. HAPPINESS

That may sound like "preacher talk," so let's see how we can have overflowing joy in—or in spite of—our trials. Notice first that the Bible does not say, "Count it all happiness." The reason is that happiness is largely driven by circumstances. It depends on what happens. If your happenings happen to be good, you'll be happy. You get a raise on the job, and you're happy. But get a pink slip, and you're sad.

In other words, happiness is basically a feeling. It is located in our emotions and subject to all their fluctuations. Our emotions cause us to react, not to think. That's why we jump in fear when the monster appears out of nowhere in a horror movie. When we do that, we are reacting to a complete fantasy that we know isn't true. But it still has the power to scare us, because emotions don't stop to take into account whether what we are seeing is true or make-believe. Our feelings respond to the information fed to them, whether it is true or not. This is not the joy that's available to us when we run into a trial.

Adding It Up

The word for "consider" in James 1:2 is a mathematical term. It means to add things up, to take an accounting of your situation. James wants you to add up the reasons for your trials, the growth and blessing that God wants to bring from them, and come up with "all joy" as the correct answer.

James is talking about divine mathematics here, because trials seldom add up or make sense if you look at them solely from the human perspective. Our first response is usually something along the lines of "Why is this happening to me, and why now? What did I do to deserve this?"

> **When God tests you, it's time to learn another lesson.**

You may not have done anything in particular to bring on the trial. James is not talking about those problems we create for ourselves by our sin and poor choices. (James 1:13–15 deals with these.) We know that from the word *encounter* (v. 2). That means something you run into, not something you bring down on your own head. We will encounter trials just by being alive. They are inescapable.

If your house is like mine, you get mail addressed to "Occupant." You don't have to be anybody or do anything to get a letter like this. It just finds you because you happen to be living in your house. I'm not suggesting that the trials God sends or allows are random. Just the opposite, in fact. What I'm saying is that all we have to do to be candidates for trials is to occupy space on this planet. Jesus told His disciples, "In the world you have tribulation, but take courage; I have overcome the world" (John 16:33).

THIS WILL BE ON THE TEST

Trials are unavoidable—but that doesn't mean they have to be unprofitable. When God tests you, it's time to learn another lesson so you can move to the next spiritual level. Like a good teacher, God tests us to prepare us for the next grade in life.

You probably remember being tested in school to see if you were ready to advance to the next grade. The bad news was that you had to take the test, but the good news was that when you passed it you demonstrated that you were ready for the next level. Of course, once you got to the next grade you also encountered a new level of testing, but that was part of the process.

God has the same purpose of growth and advancement in mind for us when He tests us. You can count it all joy that God takes the time to test you, because it means God is calling you to move on. He wants to see you succeed so you will grow.

We often complain that our trials are too hard for us, but think about it. Aren't you glad you aren't still struggling with the same temptations and obstacles you faced as a new believer (if that is truly the case)? I sincerely hope that, if you have been a Christian for some time, you have made enough spiritual progress that you can look back and say, "Oh yes, I used to really wrestle with that issue. But I've learned some valuable lessons that have made that problem seem to fade away."

Now don't misunderstand. I'm not talking about being perfect but about growing toward maturity. Can you imagine anything sadder than a forty-year-old man who is still fighting the temptation to steal change from his daddy's dresser or swipe a cookie from his mama's jar? But this is exactly where a lot of Christians are in their lives. They aren't passing God's tests, so they are stuck in kindergarten, spiritually speaking.

You need to know some other things about the trials God sends. Like a good teacher, God only tests you on information that is available to you in His Word. So if you are going through a trial, you can ask the Holy Spirit to reveal to you the truth or the lesson God wants you to know.

You also need to know that God believes in retesting until you pass. So if you don't want to be an adult sitting in a kindergartener's chair, take heed to the trial you are in and make sure you are diligently seeking God's mind on it. You can do that with confidence because James 1:3 says that God has a good purpose behind it.

OUR TRIALS ARE CUSTOM-MADE

Another important aspect of our trials and their purpose is that your trials and mine are designed with our names on them. They are custom-made. This means, for instance, that you can't say to God, "Why do I have to go through this physical suffering when Joe and all my other friends are feeling great?" Neither can Joe say to the Lord, "I don't understand why I'm struggling so hard financially and barely making it when Pete and the other guys are paying their bills easily."

Peter had this problem, as described in John 21:18–22. Jesus had risen from the dead and was restoring the disciples, and Peter in particular, to the ministry. Jesus told Peter he was going to die a martyr's death.

But Peter seemed to be more interested in the trials God had in store for John, because Peter said to Jesus, "Lord, and what about this man?" (v. 21). Jesus answered by telling Peter that John's future was none of Peter's business. "You follow Me!" (v. 22) was all that my man Pete needed to know.

IT'S IMPORTANT NOT TO QUIT

Here's one more important principle about trials before we move on. Don't get discouraged or frustrated and quit before the test is complete. Don't answer half the questions and then leave the room. James wrote, "Let endurance have its perfect result" (1:4). In other words, take the whole test or you will stunt the growth process God has built into your trial.

A little boy saw a cocoon wiggling on the side of a tree. He knew it was a butterfly struggling to emerge, and that when it came out it would be beautiful. The boy watched the struggle for a while because he wanted to see the butterfly come out and fly away, but he grew impatient as time passed.

So the little boy decided to help the butterfly, which he figured had to be exhausted by now. He broke the cocoon open, but the butterfly inside was unable to fly because its wings were not strong enough. What the boy didn't know was that the battle to shed the cocoon is necessary to develop and strengthen the butterfly's wings. The butterfly he "helped" was grounded because the boy let it out too soon.

> GOD HAS HIS HAND ON BOTH THE CLOCK AND THE THERMOSTAT IN YOUR TRIAL.

You and I will stay grounded if we don't let patience have its perfect work. You may not like your trial, and that is very natural. Jesus certainly didn't enjoy His severe trial in Gethsemane the night before His crucifixion, when His sweat became like drops of blood. But His prayer to God the Father was "Not My will, but Yours be done" (Luke 22:42).

In fact, check out the story in Luke's gospel and you will discover that Jesus' greatest moments of agony occurred *after* He had yielded His will to the Father. The Savior had to be strengthened by an angel (v. 43), and then the Bible says He sweated bloody drops (see v. 44). But He endured all the way to the cross.

My point is there's nothing wrong with feeling the pain as you endure a trial. But don't cut the trial short, or you won't get the strength that the trial is designed to deliver. Remember that God has His hand on both the clock and the thermostat in your trial, and He has promised that you will not be tempted "beyond what you are able" (1 Corinthians 10:13).

2

GOD GIVES US WISDOM TO HANDLE TRIALS

James 1:5 is a great promise that God will supply the wisdom needed to endure a trial and come out victorious on the other side. The Bible says, "But if any of you lacks wisdom [to let endurance have its perfect result], let him ask of God, who gives to all generously and without reproach, and it will be given to him."

WISDOM FOR THE HOW, NOT THE WHY

Let's not misread this promise. God is not saying that He will always answer the *why* question of your particular trial. Actually, He has already answered it by telling us that our trials are designed for our good and our growth.

So the wisdom God wants us to ask Him for is not the *why* of the trial but the *how:* that is, "Lord, I need Your wisdom to know how to react to this trial so that I am faithful to You in it and experience the growth and blessing You have for me."

Biblically, wisdom is the ability to apply divine truth to the various circumstances of life. What we need to know in our trials is the right life application to make. That's a tall order, which is why God promises us not just a trickle of divine wisdom but an overflow. God promises to answer us generously, which allows us to see the problem or the trial from His perspective and not merely from the physical realities that we observe around us.

WE NEED TO ASK IN FAITH

This promise is mind-boggling, but there's a condition attached to it. We may lack wisdom, but that's no excuse for a lack of faith. We read in James 1:6–8, "But he must ask in faith without any doubting, for the one who doubts is like the surf of the sea, driven and tossed by the wind. For that man ought not to expect that he will receive anything from the Lord, being a double-minded man, unstable in all his ways."

Being double-minded means you can't make up your mind whether you really want God's wisdom or not. You can't decide whether you want to hang in there and complete the test or bail out and take the seemingly easy road. A double-minded Christian is a schizo-phrenic saint whose divided mind and wishy-washy atti-tude don't exactly move the Lord to answer his prayer. Why? Because "without faith it is impossible to please [God], for he who comes to God must believe that He is and that He is a rewarder of those who seek Him" (Hebrews 11:6). God does not fellowship with unbelief.

But what happens too often in a trial is that we vacil-late from God to man, from the spiritual to the physical, from the human to the divine perspective. This doesn't mean we should not seek counsel from spiritually mature people, but when we are double-minded we don't elicit God's response. The reality is that far too many Chris-tians are attempting to live in both worlds, but what they wind up with is only man's view, because God says a per-son like this cannot expect anything from Him.

HOW TO BE SINGLE-MINDED

You may be saying at this point, "How about a real-life illustration of what it means to be single-minded in a trial and see God's blessing?" James took care of that for us in James 1:9–11 with an example we can all identify with: money. "The brother of humble circumstances is to glory in his high position; and the rich man is to glo-ry in his humiliation, because like flowering grass he will pass away" (vv. 9–10).

What we have here are two people in a trial involv-ing money. The poor man is scratching to make ends meet and trying to get out of the hole. The rich man either has lost most of his wealth or is experiencing a problem that is teaching him how unimportant and temporary money is in the big picture of life and how quickly riches can be swept away (see v. 11). He may have been getting too materialistic, which the phrase "the rich man in the midst of his pursuits" suggests.

In any case, what does the Bible tell both men to do? James says, "No matter whether you lack money, have all the money you need, or are in the process of losing most of your money, get your praise on." That's what "glory" means in this context. No matter what you are going through, you can praise God and be joyful when you focus on the spiritual realities of God's unfailing love for you, His firm control over the trial, and His promise of power and wisdom, not only to endure the trial but to come out victorious over it.

It Has to Go Through God

One reason the book of Job is in the Bible is to teach us that not even Satan can come against us without going through God first. Of course, there is a lot more going on in this story, but Job 1–2 reveals that the devil had to check in with God before he could touch Job. That's comforting, but the hard part for us is that God gave Satan permission to go after Job. Satan had already accused Job of serving God only because God blessed him (see Job 1:9–11).

Satan was saying that Job had it easy because he had no opposition. We don't have the space here to explore all the deep questions that the book of Job raises, but several things are inescapably clear.

First, God permitted Job to endure trials more severe than any of us will ever face. Second, Job's trials involved the opposition of Satan trying to break his faith and make him turn away from God. And third, everything that touched Job passed through God's hands first.

Why did God allow Satan to reach Job? Because God, for His own wise purposes, wanted to test Job. And in order to do that, He allowed the devil to bring adverse circumstances into Job's life. I'm not saying that every trial we undergo is the devil coming head-on at us. But we can be sure the enemy of our souls is lurking somewhere, seeking to turn a legitimate trial into a temptation to disobey God.

This difference in perspective is critical. A trial can become a temptation if we succumb to the pressure and bail out on God. It's very interesting that, in the New Testament, the same Greek word can be translated as "trial" or "temptation," depending on the context. Satan wants to turn God's trial into his own temptation, which is why we need divine wisdom to handle it.

WINNING THE CROWN OF LIFE

Now before you start feeling too heavy about all of this, let's go back to James 1 and consider this promise:

"Blessed is a man who perseveres under trial; for once he has been approved, he will receive the crown of life which the Lord has promised to those who love Him" (v. 12).

This crown is usually understood to be a reward we receive in heaven. But the context of James 1 suggests that this crown is not a reward in heaven but God's smile of approval on us in history when we endure the trial victoriously and He takes us to the next level of spiritual maturity.

We can see the crown of life being rewarded to Job at the end of his ordeal. Like a good mystery, Job has a surprise ending, because God doesn't answer the burning question of why Job underwent such intense suffering when he had done nothing wrong. Instead of answering the *why* question, God revealed Himself to Job in such an awesome display of His majesty and power that Job fell on his face.

> GOD BECOMES REAL IN THE DARKNESS.

The key to the book is found in Job 42:5, where Job confessed, "I have heard of You by the hearing of the ear; but now my eye sees You." In other words, Job had a new and infinitely deeper view of God. It's true that Job's fortune was restored and God gave him more children, but the real story in Job is that he experienced God at a level he had never known before.

Job wasn't saying he had never known God before his trial. But the revelation of God that Job had when it was over made his previous experience of God seem like child's play.

When you allow God to lead you through a trial, you get to see Him for yourself. You don't have to depend on someone else's testimony. You can take the witness stand and say, "I know He is faithful."

God becomes real in the darkness. His truth leaps off the pages of the Bible and arrests your mind and heart. God becomes so alive that it seems He is standing beside you. Does that sound like something you want? It's available to you in every trial—when you count it all joy, seek God's wisdom with a single-minded focus, and get your praise on despite the circumstances.

The next time you are in a trial, try praying this way: "God, I know You are up to something, and I can't wait to see where You are taking this thing, because I know that, whenever You send me a trial, You are ready for me to grow. So give me the strength to stay with You no matter what. Thank You for the promise of Your power and wisdom to handle this trial."

3

GOD
WANTS TO
MATURE US
THROUGH
TRIALS

It's encouraging to look at the beginning and the end of trials that biblical people like Job went through and see how God was faithful. But sometimes when we are in the middle of a hard time, we can't see where we are going, and so we can be tempted to quit or turn back in an attempt to ease the pressure.

But to do this is to fail the test and thus fail to grow toward spiritual maturity. Since we all come to a point of frustration or discouragement at one time or another, we need a word from God to exhort us and spur us on.

We have this word in the book of Hebrews, a letter written to Jewish Christians who were under the pressure of persecution and trials for their faith in Jesus Christ. The Hebrews were buckling under their circum-

stances, and they were toying with the temptation to
chuck their Christianity and go back to the familiar
ways and rituals of Judaism. As a result, they had
stopped growing and were like adults who couldn't get
past kindergarten.

The author of Hebrews wrote them in no uncertain
terms, "Don't quit! Christ is superior to anyone and anything else. There's nothing to go back to, so stop play-
ing around in kindergarten and start growing." The basic
theme of Hebrews is "Let us press on to maturity" (6:1).

This verse comes at the end of a very enlightening
section of Hebrews, which is where I want to focus as
we talk about how to acquire the maturity we need to
succeed in trials. Hebrews 5:11–14 and most of chapter
6 are a parenthesis, an aside from the author's main line
of thought. But this passage is a very important aside for
us, coming as it does in the middle of a book that was
written to urge Christians to persevere in trials.

It's Time to Grow Up

We can see from Hebrews 5:10 that the author was
getting ready to launch into an in-depth discussion of an
Old Testament priest named Melchizedek and the implications of his priesthood as a type of Jesus Christ.
The writer picked up that thought again at the end
of chapter 6, but as he prepared to teach about
Melchizedek and his relationship to Jesus, the writer realized that his readers weren't ready to plunge into the

deep end of the faith, so he pulled back to deliver an exhortation.

"Concerning him [Melchizedek] we have much to say, and it is hard to explain, since you have become dull of hearing" (5:11). The word *dull* is taken from a Greek word that means "mule-headed." It wasn't that the writer couldn't explain the teaching about Melchizedek. The problem was that the Hebrews couldn't receive it, because their spiritual comprehension had been dulled by their stubborn determination not to hear. So the subject changes in this parenthesis to the need for spiritual maturity.

The Hebrews had had time to grow and mature, because they were told, "For though by this time you ought to be teachers, you have need again for someone to teach you the elementary principles of the oracles of God, and you have come to need milk and not solid food. For everyone who partakes only of milk is not accustomed to the word of righteousness, for he is an infant. But solid food is for the mature, who because of practice have their senses trained to discern good and evil" (Hebrews 5:12–14).

The book of Hebrews was written about thirty years after Jesus' resurrection and the founding of the church on the Day of Pentecost. By this time, most of these Hebrew believers had probably been Christians long enough that they should have been in their spiritual adulthood. But that was not the case.

Growth and maturity take time. As Hebrews 5:14 says, it takes "practice" to train our senses to discern the difference between good and evil.

This basic principle has huge implications for the issue of trials. We tend to think of these as short interruptions or momentary crises that will soon pass if we can just hang in there. Thankfully, some trials do pass quickly, but many don't. A long illness or a wayward child can lead to many dark nights of the soul and body. Only God can determine how long a trial needs to last to bring us to the level of new growth He wants us to achieve.

We Can Speed Our Spiritual Growth

The speed at which you go determines how fast you will grow. We know from James 1:4 that God's purpose for our trials is that we grow until we are "perfect and complete," or fully mature.

This is where the analogy between physical and spiritual growth breaks down, because it is possible to grow spiritually at an accelerated rate. That's why we see some five-year-old Christians who are more mature than others who have been saved for thirty years.

As a pastor, I've seen this principle lived out in many people's lives through the trials they undergo. For example, two families will experience severe financial trials. The first family will, by their own testimony, recognize that they have not been good stewards of the resources God gave them, and the Holy Spirit convicts them of the need to transfer their trust from money to their Lord. They learn the lesson, start giving to God first, and He turns their situation around.

I'm not saying that, if you give to God, all of your financial worries will be over and you will be prosperous. That's the message you get from some preachers, not from God's Word. But God does honor those who honor Him.

What about the second family in my illustration? These are the folk who just don't get it. I can't count how many times I've had people tell me, "Pastor, I know I'm supposed to be giving to the Lord, but I can't afford to right now." They often go on to tell me how they were going to start giving that very month, but the refrigerator or the car broke down.

Of course, emergencies happen to all of us. The problem with these people is that once the car is fixed, something else comes up to keep them from being obedient to God. I'm talking about believers who have been doing this dance for years and still haven't grown to the point that they can trust God completely. So God is faithful to keep retesting them.

I have a friend who says his situation didn't turn around until he and his wife made an absolute, irrevocable commitment to honor the Lord first even if it meant they didn't have enough money left over to eat or pay the house note. That hasn't happened, although they've had the usual car problems, broken appliances, and other emergencies along the way.

I should mention that this illustration works the other way too. Many Christians have testified that even though they were doing quite well financially without honoring God, they paid a heavy price in terms of a ruined marriage, ill health, lost peace of mind, serious family problems, or some painful combination thereof. And in many cases, when they persisted in their lack of faith, God eventually allowed their financial house to come tumbling down.

This issue of our spiritual growth rate is serious, especially in relation to our trials. The Hebrews had been Christians long enough that the writer could say, "By this time you ought to be teachers" (5:12), because one of the evidences of growth is your ability to help someone else grow.

But instead, they were still trying to learn the ABCs of the Christian faith (that's the basic meaning of "the elementary principles of the oracles of God," v. 12b). But there is more: "And you have come to need milk and not solid food" (v. 12c).

The Difference Between Milk and Meat

Milk and solid food (also translated "meat," the term I want to use here) are the diet of babies and adults, respectively (see Hebrews 5:13–14). Babies can't take meat because their systems are not mature enough to digest it. The same principle is true in the spiritual realm. There's nothing wrong with a baby's needing milk, but these Hebrew believers weren't babies—at least in relation to their spiritual age. But they were still taking their spiritual nourishment from a bottle.

As used in passages like this, the term *milk* is generally understood to represent the basic, "easier" doctrines of the faith, such as sin and salvation, while meat is the "deeper" or harder-to-understand parts of the Scriptures. In this view, John 3:16 would be milk, while the Melchizedek high priesthood of Jesus would be meat. Thus, to grow from drinking milk to eating meat would be to move from a beginner's understanding of the faith to a deep grasp of Bible doctrine.

The problem with limiting milk and meat to this concept is that there is more to these terms. If spiritual growth were simply a matter of content, then the more Bible we know, the more spiritual we will be. But this isn't always true. There are Christians who know more Bible than others but are not as spiritual as those who know less than they do.

That's because the difference between milk and meat goes deeper than a difference in the amount of Bible knowledge people have in their heads. Let's define milk and meat as they are biblically understood. They involve not just the learning of Bible doctrine, but the application of Bible doctrine. Hebrews 6:1–2 says, "Therefore leaving the elementary teaching about the Christ, let us press on to maturity, not laying again a foundation of repentance from dead works and of faith toward God, of instruction about washings and laying on of hands, and the resurrection of the dead and eternal judgment."

In a word, milk is *understanding* what the Bible says,

whereas meat is understanding and *applying* what the Bible says. When you understand what God is telling you in His Word, when you comprehend what it means and what it requires, you have a delicious glass of milk. Nothing wrong with that, because milk is nourishing. It's just not enough by itself to keep you growing past infancy.

To keep growing you need meat, or solid food. But digesting solid food takes more concentrated effort because it must be chewed thoroughly. It doesn't go down as easily as milk. To put it in spiritual terms, you can go to all the Bible classes and seminars in the world and read every Christian book or booklet around, including this one. But no matter how much truth you take in, if it doesn't produce greater righteousness and Christlikeness in your life, you are only drinking milk.

IT TAKES PRACTICE

What does it take to transform that milk into meat, the solid food that builds strong spirits the way physical food builds strong bodies? The answer is back in Hebrews 5:14. It takes the kind of "practice" that leads to our being "trained," which in this context is a synonym for being mature.

But this process takes time. So in terms of our trials, we have come full circle. God wants us to emerge from our trials more mature than when we started. But that means we must spend time in the trial, because God is not going to rush the process. He wants us to "practice" enduring trials so we will be fully trained and ready to go.

When the risen Christ delivered His message to the seven churches of Asia in Revelation 2–3, He ended each message with the admonition "He who has an ear, let him hear what the Spirit says to the churches." Jesus didn't want His people just to learn the words on the page. He wanted their spiritual senses to become so well trained that they could perceive what the Holy Spirit was saying to them and adjust their lives accordingly.

> WHEN GOD SENDS US A TRIAL, IT'S A PRACTICE SESSION.

The Holy Spirit's job is to apply divine truth to your life so you can make godly decisions between good and bad, right and wrong. Maturity is the ability to make decisions with the truth, not just recite the truth. Where there is no ability to make decisions, there is no maturity.

As I write this, my son Jonathan plays football for Baylor University. He called me one day and said, "Well, Dad, I just thought I'd call you and say hi because I won't be able to call you again for a while."

When I asked him why, he said, "Because the coaches are confiscating our phones and car keys and taking us to a private place to stay. They are going to bus us to the field for practice in the morning, bring us back to study the playbook, then take us back to the field in the afternoon to work on what we went over in class."

In other words, the coaches don't trust that just because the players heard it in class, they have it. They take them out to practice, where they have to execute it on the field over and over and over again. Why? Because when Baylor faces Nebraska or Texas, they can't say, "Time out, let me check the playbook on this one." They have to have their senses trained to react. It's got to be an automatic reaction. And players only get that from practicing until it becomes second nature.

God does the same thing with us. When God sends us a trial, it's a practice session. He is calling us to put into practice on Monday the truth we said "Amen" to on Sunday.

Let me take this analogy one important step further. The reason a football team works so hard to execute its plays is that in the real game there is another team on the other side of the ball resisting every move the team makes. Teams don't practice for the sake of practice. They practice knowing that they will face opposition in the real game.

In the same way, God wants us to practice righteousness until our senses are well trained and we are mature, because the world, our own sinful flesh, and the devil are waiting to resist us. We are on our way to spiritual maturity when the information we take in (milk) is translated into our daily practice (meat). This is the essence of spiritual maturity, and it's what God is after when He sends trials our way.

4

WE CAN TRUST GOD THROUGH TRIALS

You may be saying at this point, "God sure expects a lot from us in our trials." He does, but there is nothing God expects that He has not supplied us with the power to accomplish. And best of all, we can trust God to bring us through our trials. Sometimes we just need the proper motivation to hang in there and triumph over trials.

Speaking of the proper motivation, I heard about a man who was walking home late one chilly, rainy night. He was so tired and cold that he decided to take a short-cut through the town cemetery. Unfortunately, he didn't see an open grave and fell headlong into the hole. He panicked, clawing at the sides of the grave and hollering for help. But after a while it became apparent that no one was around, and he couldn't get enough of a grip to climb out. He was so exhausted that he huddled down in one side of the dark grave and fell asleep.

As it turned out, another man was walking through the cemetery in the wee hours of the morning. He also fell into the open grave and, like the first man, began yelling for help and trying to climb out. His shouts woke the first man, who was hidden from sight in the darkness. The first man reached out, laid a cold, clammy hand on the second man's shoulder, and said, "Forget it, brother. You'll never make it. I've been trying to get out of here for hours." The second man made it!

THERE IS A GREAT CLOUD ABOVE US

With the proper motivation, we can do almost anything. The recipients of the letter to the Hebrews needed the right motivation in their trials, which is why the author went through God's Hall of Faith in chapter 11 and pointed to some Old Testament examples of people who won out over their trials with God's help. Then the author came back with his best word of encouragement, motivation, and admonition in Hebrews 12:1–3:

> Therefore, since we have so great a cloud of witnesses surrounding us, let us also lay aside every encumbrance and the sin which so easily entangles us, and let us run with endurance the race that is set before us, fixing our eyes on Jesus, the author and perfecter of faith, who for

the joy set before Him endured the cross, despising the shame, and has sat down at the right hand of the throne of God. For consider Him who has endured such hostility by sinners against Himself, so that you will not grow weary and lose heart.

The point of Hebrews 12:1 is that if God could keep His eye on Abraham when he left everything he knew to move to a strange land and live in tents, then God won't lose track of you. If God could sustain Moses when he left the pleasures and wealth of Egypt for the life of a lowly shepherd, then God can sustain you. You are not out there by yourself. Men and women of God have been living by faith in some of the most trying of circumstances, and since Jesus is the same today as He was yesterday (see Hebrews 13:8), we can trust Him to keep us by His power. You can trust God in your trials.

OUR FAITH TAPS GOD'S POWER

Trusting God when we can't see where He's taking us, or when it looks as if we're heading toward a cliff, is an act of faith. Faith is the subject of Hebrews 11, as we are told in the very first verse: "Faith is the assurance of things hoped for, the conviction of things not seen."

Faith is simply believing God, having absolute assurance that He is completely truthful in everything He says. Faith has definite content, even though that content may be unseen. The issue in faith is always the object of our faith, not faith in faith itself. God calls us to have faith in an object that is big enough and worthy enough to merit our trust—His own person and promises.

Some things just aren't worthy of our trust. For my wife, small airplanes fit into that category. I had a speaking engagement one time in a place that was hard to reach by a commercial airliner. So our hosts told us they were going to send a four-seat private plane to pick up my wife and me. But she wasn't buying it. "There is no way you are going to get me in a little airplane like that! I am not going."

I tried to talk her into it, but she wasn't about to board that plane. So I used my preacher approach and said, "You don't have enough faith."

But she said, "No, you don't have enough airplane."

We worked it out so that we could travel on a commercial airline, and my wife went with me. I said to her, "I see that your faith grew."

"That's because your airplane grew."

The reason many of us have small faith, especially when we are going through trials, is that we have a small God. That's why the most important doctrine for a Christian to understand is the doctrine of God, because your view of God will determine the size of your faith.

Faith is being persuaded that God always tells the truth. So when He says, "I will never desert you, nor will I ever forsake you" (Hebrews 13:5), you can take that promise to the bank. By the way, it's no coincidence that this verse comes at the end of Hebrews. The author had been saying, "Do not turn your back on Christ and walk away," and then he closed by saying, "You can make it, because God will never turn His back on you and walk away."

God never asks anyone to act on so-called blind faith. The message of Hebrews 11 is that many people took God at His word and triumphed even when things were at their

> MANY CHRISTIANS ARE FAITH TALKERS, NOT FAITH WALKERS.

toughest. The heroes of Hebrews 11 can say to us, "We've been where you are going, we have fought and won the battle, and we can tell you that God is faithful."

HOW TO KEEP JESUS IN OUR FOCUS

It's great to have someone tell us that we can make it, too. But don't miss the bottom line of Hebrews 11–12. We are to fix our eyes on Jesus, not on the people who have gone before us. We look at them, but we focus on Jesus.

The truth is that too many Christians are more willing to put their faith in another human being than they are in God. We trust doctors, pharmacists, and all manner of other people when they tell us that what they are giving us is good for us. We can't even read the prescription our doctor gives us, but we make a faith decision to take this medicine we know nothing about.

Many Christians are faith talkers, not faith walkers. And as we saw earlier, "without faith it is impossible to please Him" (Hebrews 11:6).

It reminds me of the farming community that was in such a terrible drought the farmers were in danger of losing their crops. The situation was so bad that the pastors called a special prayer meeting to pray for rain. Everyone came to the meeting with their Bibles and prayed for rain for two hours. But nothing happened, so everyone went home.

Everyone, that is, except for a boy in the back. He walked outside, looked up, and said, "Lord, we need rain. We are in a crisis, and You promised to meet our needs. So we are expecting it to rain." Soon the clouds began to form, and, before long, rain started falling. The boy's face broke into a huge smile, and he pulled out the umbrella he had brought to the prayer meeting, opened it up, and walked home. The others said they believed in God, but this boy acted as if he believed in God.

If you feel like you're in a drought in your trial, have you come to God with your umbrella in hand, ready to hear from heaven? If we are living faithless lives, we are displeasing to God. God is not happy with us when we fail to trust Him, because nothing can take the place of faith.

We are surrounded by a cloud of witnesses who affirm the fact that God is telling the truth when He promises to take us through whatever we may face. You can win whatever battle or crisis you are in right now because you can trust God in your trial. And you have a great cloud of witnesses from the past to remind you that you serve the same changeless, eternally faithful God.

LET'S GET IN THE RACE

It's great to sit in the stands and cheer others who are winning the game. But we have to get in the game ourselves—or run our own race, to use the imagery of Hebrews 12:1. We can't just run any old way we please, either. Look at the Bible's instructions to us.

Since we are surrounded by these witnesses, our challenge is to "lay aside every encumbrance and the sin which so easily entangles us." What sin has the power to entangle the body of Christ and cause all of us to stumble? Well, the context of these verses is the need for faith, so the sin that so easily entangles us is the sin of unbelief. Unbelief is so potent that it kept the entire nation of Israel, around two million people, out of the Promised Land for forty years.

Moses had delivered God's word of deliverance and salvation to Israel in Egypt, and the people saw God's miraculous power lead them out of their severe trial of slavery. But when the moment came to step over the line and into the Promised Land, the people turned back.

What went wrong? The book of Hebrews tells us, because the writer was trying to keep these believers from committing the same sin of unbelief by turning back from following God. According to Hebrews 4:2, the word of God that the Israelites heard "did not profit them, because it was not united by faith in those who heard."

WE HAVE TO HAVE THE RIGHT MIX

I like the translation "not being mixed with faith" (KJV). You can anchor a child's swing set, a basketball goal, a fence post, or anything else you want with cement, but it has to be mixed with water to form concrete. If you are in a shaky situation and you need an anchor for your soul, you need to mix God's truth with your faith. That is, you need to act as if God will provide you with the strength to bear your trial.

Hebrews 12:1 says that once we get rid of the sin of unbelief that gets us tangled up so easily, we can run the race "with endurance." This agrees with what James said about our trials: "Let endurance have its perfect result" (James 1:4). Keep going; don't quit.

You say, "But I'm tired." That's all right, God will give you grace to press on for one more day tomorrow, and then He will meet you with grace to endure the day after tomorrow. We need to hear Jesus' command in this regard: "Do not worry about tomorrow; for tomorrow will care for itself" (Matthew 6:34). You may not see anything but the crisis right now, but God's Word assures you that Christ is in your crisis. And that's all any of us really needs to know.

That's why we are told in Hebrews 12:2 to keep our

eyes on Jesus. He is the "author," or architect, of our faith and the "perfecter," or completer, of our faith—which also means that He is everything in between the start and the finish of this race called the Christian life. The time to look to the Savior is not just when things are going well and you are singing praises, but when the pain is the most intense and you feel like you are going to collapse any minute.

Unafraid of the Furnace

Do you remember the three Hebrew boys of Daniel 3? They were captives of King Nebuchadnezzar of Babylon, so I think that qualifies as a trial. The king had made a golden image and decreed that everyone in Babylon bow down and worship it. But these three Jewish young men could not do that without violating God's commandment to worship no other god, so they refused.

Now old King Nebby thought he held the trump card: "If you will not worship, you will immediately be cast into the midst of a furnace of blazing fire; and what god is there who can deliver you out of my hands?" (Daniel 3:15).

As far as the king was concerned, the only options were to bow or burn. But that didn't ruffle those Hebrew boys, because they had a third option: believe. I love what they said to the king: "O Nebuchadnezzar, we do not need to give you an answer concerning this matter" (v. 16; see also vv. 17–18).

In other words, "This is going to be very quick. We don't even need to think about it, Your Highness. We discussed this before we ever took this job, and we agreed that if the choice came down to our God or you, Nebby, you lose. If our God wants to, He can deliver us from your fiery furnace because He is able to do that. But even if He doesn't, and we roast to death in there, He's still the only God, and we aren't going to worship your fool image" (Evans paraphrase).

Now please don't skip over that opening phrase in verse 18: "But even if He does not [deliver us from the fire]." We love to hear the part about how God delivered the three Hebrew children from the fiery furnace and later delivered Daniel from the lions' den. And that's OK, because those are exciting examples of God's power to deliver His people from the worst trials we can imagine.

> TRUSTING GOD WILL KEEP YOU FROM BEING IN YOUR CRISIS ALONE.

But the point of Daniel 3:18 is that these three young men realized that God might not choose to deliver them in the way they hoped. They understood that if they defied the king and trusted God, they might get tossed into the furnace and come out as shish kebabs. But whatever God chose was fine with them, because they believed He would act on their behalf, and they put their faith into action when all they had to do to avoid a death sentence was dip their knee for a second to the king.

When you fix your eyes on Jesus and begin acting as if what He said is true, you are in a win-win situation. Even if you come out of your next fiery furnace trial feet first, "to be absent from the body [is] to be at home with the Lord" (2 Corinthians 5:8). You can't lose with Christ.

WITH GOD, THERE ARE FOUR

My friend, I can't promise you that trusting God will get you out of your crisis. But I *can* promise you that trusting God will keep you from being in your crisis alone. The Bible says that a fourth figure joined those Hebrew boys in Nebby's furnace (see Daniel 3:25).

I believe that when the three Hebrews were in the furnace, they were not moping around. I'm guessing they were singing the songs of Zion. They had the joy of the Lord, which Jesus had even in the shadow of the cross. "The joy of the Lord is your strength" (Nehemiah 8:10).

The author of Hebrews said of Jesus, "Who for the joy set before Him endured the cross" (12:2). The cross was not something Jesus wanted to endure. But He fixed His eyes on His Father in heaven and the joy that would be His when He had accomplished the Father's will perfectly, redeemed hopeless sinners like us, and came out of the grave triumphantly three days later.

Hebrews 12:2 goes on to say that when Jesus had

endured the cross, He "sat down at the right hand of the throne of God." Now, that's exciting enough, because it means Jesus finished His work of redemption and is enthroned in heaven. Then we read in verse 3, "Consider Him who has endured such hostility by sinners against Himself, so that you will not grow weary and lose heart."

Let me show you something that I hope will put some steel in your backbone and some joy in your heart as you endure the trials of life. The Bible not only says that Jesus is seated at the right hand of God in heaven, but also that we are seated with Jesus "in the heavenly places" (Ephesians 2:6).

This is not just something we will enjoy someday when we get to heaven. This is our present reality as believers. So if you feel as if you are about to lose heart in your trial, before you give up, look up and see Jesus seated at God's right hand. And because you are there with Him, you have access to all that God the Father has for you. Jesus sat down because He finished His race—His work as our Savior. And now His power, joy, and grace are available to help us finish our race. Keep your eyes on Jesus, the author and perfecter of your faith.

5

WE CAN LAY A FOUNDATION THAT CAN WITHSTAND ANY TRIAL

One section of the city of Dallas is undergoing an amazing transformation. The construction project is a piece of freeway design and engineering called the "High Five" project, because when it's all done in a couple more years, there will be five levels of overpasses to relieve congestion and keep traffic flowing at a place where two of the city's busiest freeways intersect.

This thing is really incredible to see going up. There will be more than eight hundred huge concrete pillars supporting the overpasses, and that fifth level looks like it is going to be high enough to give a driver a nosebleed.

Now, I enjoy driving, and I like a good adventure, but I'll tell you something. Before I go up on the fifth level of road, I want to know that the workers didn't skimp on the concrete foundations supporting the roadbed. Approaching the peak of an overpass that's hanging high in the air, especially if the wind is blowing hard, is a very poor time to discover that the foundation under you is shaky.

Being buffeted by the winds of a difficult trial is also a poor time to discover that your spiritual foundation is shaky. So I want to finish this booklet by helping you lay a solid foundation for your life that will enable you to withstand any test or trial that the world, the flesh, or the devil can throw at you. I have the best possible "architect" for the job too—Jesus Christ Himself.

HOW FIRM IS YOUR FOUNDATION?

Jesus finished the greatest sermon ever preached, the Sermon on the Mount, with one of the best-known stories in all of the Bible. He told of two men who built houses on different foundations, and He described what happened to each man's house:

> Therefore everyone who hears these words of Mine and acts on them, may be compared to a wise man who built his house on the rock. And the rain fell, and the floods came, and the winds blew and slammed against that house; and yet it did not fall, for it had been founded on the rock. Everyone who hears these words of Mine and does not act on them, will be like a foolish man who built

his house on the sand. The rain fell, and the floods came, and the winds blew and slammed against that house; and it fell—and great was its fall. (Matthew 7:24–27)

You've heard of a tale of two cities. Well, here we have a tale of two men. They had a lot in common, but they had one very crucial difference that formed the crux of Jesus' story.

Let's notice their similarities first. Each man had the same dream: Each wanted to build a house for his family. In the Bible the imagery of building a house is used in several different contexts. It can refer to building an individual life. Building a house could also refer to a person's family. Psalm 127 gives us the formula for building a house that the Lord can bless, but the psalmist is talking about far more than just erecting a physical structure. He's talking about how to build a spiritually strong family. We can assume that the two men in Matthew 7 also wanted to build successful lives and families.

But even more than that, we could say that they both had the same pastor. Jesus said that both men heard His words. They both listened to the same pulpiteer, and there is no better preacher than Jesus. So both men were exposing themselves to the truth of God, from the very mouth of God.

But the similarities between these two men faded into the background when the storm hit, for the wind and the waves revealed the one critical difference between them—a different foundation to their houses and lives. This difference is so major that Jesus called the first man "wise" and labeled the second man "foolish." We need to consider these terms.

HOW TO AVOID A FOOLISH FOUNDATION

The wise person can bring what God says to bear on the decision-making process and arrive at a God-honoring conclusion. Someone has described wisdom as the skill of biblical living. The first man in Jesus' story had this ability.

But Jesus called the other man "foolish," a Greek word that means "moron." A fool in the Bible is not someone who lacks cognitive ability but a person with a complete lack of biblical comprehension and discernment, and thus a complete lack of skill in living. And what's worse, the fool often doesn't even recognize his foolishness so that he can correct it.

The difference between the two men in Matthew 7 showed up in their approach to building their houses. The wise man built his house on a foundation called "the rock," or Jesus Himself. Luke's gospel says he "dug deep" (Luke 6:48). But the foolish man built his house on the sand.

Why would anyone build a house on something as unstable as sand? It could be that he wanted to save a few bucks. Rocky foundations are more costly than sand. Maybe the foolish man also wanted to save some hard work and time by opting for an easier foundation.

You really can't do anything to prepare a foundation in sand, because if you try to dig deep the sand will cave in. That's why people in Florida don't have basements.

In other words, the foolish man wanted the cheap and easy way out. He did not want to pay the cost or take the time to lay a strong foundation to his house.

You can tell how high construction workers are going to go with a building by how deep they go into the ground for the foundation. The foundation must be worthy of the structure being built, or someone is in for trouble. One of the images I will never forget from 9/11 is the enormous hole at Ground Zero, which shows the massive size of the foundations that undergirded the twin towers of the World Trade Center in New York.

You can't build a high building without going low first. It amazes me how, in the spiritual realm, many people who want to soar high aren't willing to go low first. I'm talking about taking the time and effort to lay a solid foundation in their lives through the disciplines of the Word, prayer, worship, witnessing, fasting, and the other facets of the Christian life.

Here's a tip that will save you money if you ever travel to Italy. Skip the Tower of Pisa. I was never so disappointed as I was when I saw this tiny little building leaning sideways. That's all there was to it. But at least the Tower of Pisa is good to illustrate the value of building on the right foundation.

The tower leans because Pisa is marshy land. In fact, the word *pisa* means "marshy." The tower was built on mud without the right foundation, and one side of it began to sink in the marsh. It was even in danger of falling down a few years ago, so they had to reinforce it.

The foolish man in Jesus' story built the "leaning house of Galilee," so to speak, and it crashed when the storm came. But the wise man made it through the storm, or trial, and the only contrast between them was their foundations.

PUTTING GOD'S WORD TO WORK

What made the all-important difference? Jesus said it was the difference between just hearing His words and putting them into practice. Both men had half of the proper ingredients for a firm foundation. They both heard Jesus' words. Both men went to church and sat under the Word, to put it in today's terms. But the first man took the Word home with him and applied it, while the second man left what he heard on the pew along with his crumpled bulletin when he left church.

> IF JESUS IS YOUR FOUNDATION, YOU'LL BE ABLE TO WITHSTAND THE STORM.

The first man acted from a divine standpoint, while his neighbor with the nice house on the beach operated from a human standpoint. I don't know if you have ever noticed, but a human viewpoint is very sandy. Sand shifts and drifts according to whichever way the wind is blowing at the moment.

A human viewpoint is one that allows a person to believe whatever the television tells him to believe. A human viewpoint may make a person feel comfortable for a while, but when the tide of life comes in, it gets swept away.

You see, the issue of whether we are wise or foolish people is not what church we attend or how often we attend. It has to do with what we do with God's truth. You may know how to recite the Word, but do you apply the truth you have memorized, because you believe that God has spoken and He has not stuttered?

Hearing God's Word is not enough. The apostle James said it is not the "forgetful hearer" but the "effectual doer" who will be blessed in what he does (James 1:25).

Here Is the Bottom Line

If I were preaching right now I might say, "And in conclusion," at this point, because this is where I want to focus your attention. The storm that battered the two houses in Jesus' story did not determine the two men's foundations; it only exposed them.

This storm wasn't a summer shower. The rains and wind blew hard enough to knock down a house. This was the kind of storm that breaks windows and makes the roof lift and heave. When you encounter a storm like this, you'd better have the right foundation.

If Jesus is your foundation, you'll be able to withstand the storm. But let me tell you a secret. If He isn't your foundation, you need to get started pouring a new one today, because you can't lay a foundation when it's pouring rain. You can pour a solid foundation before or after a storm, but not during. The middle of a crisis is a terrible time to discover that your house is shaking and shuddering as the foundation washes away.

JESUS IS THERE—NO MATTER WHAT

Someone may be saying today, "Well, I thought Jesus was my foundation. But I'm not so sure right now, because I'm being battered by this trial, and it feels like my life is going to give way under me. I'm scared to death, and, in fact, to be really honest I've kind of been wondering if Jesus really knows what I'm going through."

If you have ever felt that way, you are not alone. Many Christians have had the same questions in the storm, which is why I want to take you to Mark 4:35–41, a real-life episode with Jesus and His disciples.

On this particular day, Jesus put the disciples in a boat and said, "Let us go over to the other side," meaning the other side of the Sea of Galilee. They started out, but a huge storm came up suddenly, and they were in trouble. The Greek word for this storm emphasizes that it came out of nowhere, one of those completely unexpected storms that the Sea of Galilee was famous for.

Now, the disciples were experienced on the water, but they panicked this time. They had begun bailing water when someone figured out, "Hey, wait a minute. Jesus is with us." So they looked around, but when they saw Jesus they became a little "evangelically ticked off," because Jesus was asleep in the stern of the boat (see v. 38).

The disciples were upset. What good was having Jesus on your boat if He was asleep when you needed Him most? What good is having a Deliverer who is not delivering you from the storm? So the disciples stirred Jesus awake and asked this accusing question: "Teacher, do You not care that we are perishing?" (v. 38). In other words, "Jesus, we hate to bother You, but we could use a little help here. If You really care about us, get up and do something."

We can sit in church and sing the old hymn that asks, "Does Jesus care?" about the things that happen to us. That hymn gives the resounding answer, "O yes, He cares, I know He cares." But when your house is being battered or your boat is filling with water, the temptation is to say, "Hello, anyone out there? Jesus, if You really cared about me You'd be doing something. I'm bailing, but You're sleeping."

GOD HASN'T FORGOTTEN YOU

Jesus got up and stilled the storm. That was the easy part. Then He turned to the Twelve and said, "Why are you afraid? How is it that you have no faith?" (Mark 4:40).

Jesus' question seems a little harsh, given their current reality. But He said it because His men had forgotten what He said before they ever got in the boat: "Let us go over to the other side." He did not intend for His disciples to go out halfway in the water and drown.

The Twelve had heard Jesus say this, but in the middle of their crisis they forgot what He said. The Word was not abiding in them. The storm was now determining their theology. Jesus cared about them, but they lost sight of that fact.

When you seem to be drowning, remember what Jesus said.

Whenever it looks like your God has gone to sleep on you, know that He has a purpose in mind. He hasn't forgotten where you are, and He hasn't stopped caring. He wants to see what you are going to do with His Word when the storm hits.

And make no mistake; it is going to rain. The storms will come. It's been aptly said that you are either coming out of a storm, in a storm, or headed toward a storm. It is going to rain. After Jesus stilled the storm, the disciples became afraid of Him (Mark 4:41). That's OK. If you are going to fear something, fear Jesus, not the wind or the rain.

Did Jesus know that storm was coming? Of course. Did He send the disciples into it on purpose? Yes, He did. Why? To teach them the same lesson we need to learn over and over again. When you have Jesus, you have a foundation that is built with the storms of life in mind. Nothing surprises or overwhelms Him. With Jesus as the foundation of your life, you can endure the batterings that life brings. Nothing can capsize your boat when Jesus is in it.

God has already determined what is going to come your way, and He is sufficient for it. But you must learn to absorb and apply His Word. God has been truthful in telling us that the trials are sure to come. And He has given us everything we need in His Word and the indwelling presence of the Holy Spirit to bring that Word to our remembrance and help us apply it.

When I was a boy, my father bought me one of those balloon punching bags with a wide base. No matter how hard or how many times I hit that bag, it kept popping back up because it was well anchored at the bottom. It had a foundation that was stronger than my hardest punch.

Sometimes life is going to hit you with a balled-up fist, and you may sway. But if Jesus and His Word are your anchor, your foundation, you are going to come back. Sometimes Satan is going to hit you, but if Christ and His Word are your foundation, you will come back, even though you may rock a little bit. How do I know? Because "greater is He who is in you than he who is in the world" (1 John 4:4).

Since 1894, Moody Publishers has been dedicated to equip and motivate people to advance the cause of Christ by publishing evangelical Christian literature and other media for all ages, around the world. Because we are a ministry of the Moody Bible Institute of Chicago, a portion of the proceeds from the sale of this book go to train the next generation of Christian leaders.

If we may serve you in any way in your spiritual journey toward understanding Christ and the Christian life, please contact us at www.moodypublishers.com.

"All Scripture is God-breathed and is useful for teaching, rebuking, correcting and training in righteousness, so that the man of God may be thoroughly equipped for every good work."
—2 TIMOTHY 3:16, 17

MOODY
PUBLISHERS

THE NAME YOU CAN TRUST®

More from Tony Evans and Moody Publishers

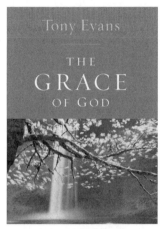

ISBN: 0-8024-4380-X

Everyone in this world has a debt—a spiritual debt to God. And yet, if we accept His grace, he cancels the debt—everyone can relate to this. God's grace can be a difficult-to-understand subject, but Tony Evans makes it clear and easy-to-digest.

The Grace of God focuses on five clear elements:
   —The Concept of Grace
   —Saved by Grace
   —Sanctified by Grace
   —Set Free by Grace
   —Sufficiency of Grace

Read on as Tony Evans explores the meaning and practical application of grace: unearned, undeserved kindness

MOODY
PUBLISHERS

THE NAME YOU CAN TRUST.

1-800-678-6928 www.MoodyPublishers.org

CAN GOD BE TRUSTED? TEAM

ACQUIRING EDITOR
Greg Thornton

DEVELOPMENT EDITOR
Phil Rawley

COPY EDITOR
Cheryl Dunlop

BACK COVER COPY
Elizabeth Cody Newenhuyse

COVER DESIGN
Smartt Guys

COVER PHOTO
John Foxx/Alamy Images

INTERIOR DESIGN
Ragont Design

PRINTING AND BINDING
Versa Press Inc.

The typeface for the text of this book is
Weiss